Weekly Reader PRESENTS

Be An Inventor

by Barbara Taylor

Harcourt Brace Jovanovich, Publishers

San Diego   New York   London

*To all the young people whose ideas
will be the inventions of tomorrow*

Copyright © 1987 by Field Publications

All rights reserved. No part of this publication may be reproduced or transmitted in any form or by any means, electronic or mechanical, including photocopy, recording, or any information storage and retrieval system, without permission in writing from the publisher.

Requests for permission to make copies of any part of the work should be mailed to:
Permissions, Harcourt Brace Jovanovich, Publishers, Orlando, Florida 32887.

Photography Credits
AT&T—p. 45 (top); *Aurora Advertiser*/Paul E. Donley—p. 5 (bottom); The Bettmann Archive—pp. iv (top), 39, 40 (top right and bottom), 46 (bottom); Bissell Inc.—p. 41 (all); Borden—pp. 42, 43 (both); *The Capital Times*/Henry A. Koshollek—p. 5 (top); Culver—p. 31; General Foods—pp. 37, 38; Gillette Company Safety Razor Division—pp. 54, 55; Granger Collection—p. 46 (top); Herral Long—pp. 34–36; IBM—p. 15 (top right); NASA—pp. 11–13; *People Weekly* © 1986 Time Inc./ Wm. Franklin McMahon—p. 3; Charles Phillips, Smithsonian Book Dept.—p. 17; Procter and Gamble Company—pp. 32, 33; Schomburg Center, N.Y. Public Library—p. 26; Myron Starbird—p. 24; Submarine Force Museum, Groton, CT—p. v; Texas Instruments, Inc.—pp. 14, 15 (bottom left); UPI—pp. 27, 28 (both), 47; U.S. Dept. of the Interior, National Park Service, Edison National Historic Site—p. 48; U.S. Patent and Trademark Office—pp. 19–21, 29, 40 (top left), 61–63, 65–67; Wide World—pp. vi, 15 (bottom right), 30 (both).

Library of Congress Cataloging-in-Publication Data

   Taylor, Barbara (Barbara Talbot)
   Be an inventor.

   Bibliography: p.
   At head of title: Weekly reader presents.
   Summary: A manual, designed to inspire inventive thinking, with descriptions of a variety of inventions and information on patenting, marketing, and selling one's inventions.
   1. Inventions—Juvenile literature. [1. Inventions]
I. Title.
T48.T37   1987   608   87-12051
ISBN   0-15-205950-4
ISBN   0-15-205951-2 (pbk.)

Designed by Janet Kanca
Printed in the United States of America
First edition
A B C D E
A B C D E (pbk.)

Contents

Introduction v
1 Introducing *Weekly Reader*'s Young Inventors 1
2 What Makes a Person "Inventive"? 9
3 Strange and Unusual Inventions 19
4 A Behind-the-Scenes Look at Some Inventions ... 22
5 Getting Started 37
6 Thinking Like an Inventor 52
7 What's a Patent? 61
8 Selling Your Invention 68
9 More Help with Inventions 71
   Suggested Reading 72
   Acknowledgments 73

Marconi (above) with his first experimental wireless set. Even as a boy, Marconi was completely devoted to his research on the wireless. He sometimes tried to save time by skipping meals, a practice that tested his father's patience.

Alexander Graham Bell (right) at the age of 16. By the age of 29, he had invented the telephone. In later years, he helped develop numerous inventions, from a hydrofoil boat to air conditioning.

Introduction

- Guglielmo Marconi was just 8 years old when he figured out how to make ink from berries he gathered in his father's garden. By the time he was 21, Marconi had invented the wireless radio, which could send messages across oceans.

- David Bushnell began work on one of the world's first successful submarines when he was still a teenager. Years later, he piloted his submarine, the *Turtle,* against the British during the American Revolution.

- Sixteen-year-old Alexander Graham Bell designed a rubber doll's head that could say "Mama." What he learned from this early invention later helped Bell to invent the telephone.

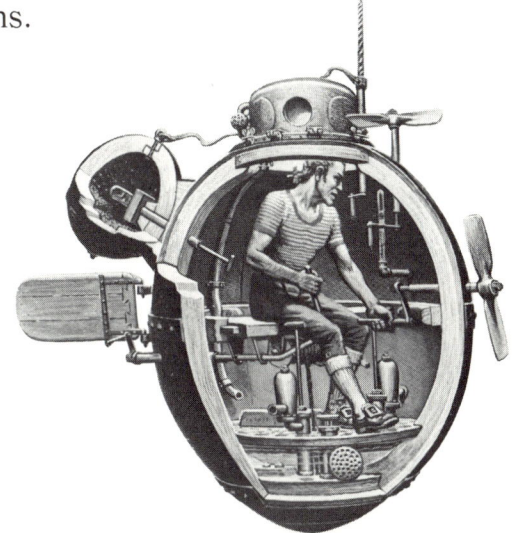

A drawing of the inside of David Bushnell's Turtle

Some of the world's greatest inventors, like Marconi, Bushnell, and Bell, got started when they were your age or a little older. They were inventors even though they were very young, for age is not really important when it comes to inventing. What *is* important is curiosity, imagination, confidence, and a willingness to work at solving problems. If you have these qualities, *you* can be an inventor.

You may have already had an idea for an invention. Why not turn your idea into reality?

Seventh-grader Matthew Peters won a grand prize for inventing the **S.I.T. Skoot** *after he watched his dad skate fast and then sit on his hockey stick and glide over the ice. Matthew's invention works in a similar way. It consists of a pole and wheels. The pole is held between the legs and the wheels roll over ice or other smooth surfaces.*

CHAPTER 1

Introducing *Weekly Reader's* Young Inventors

Weekly Reader, *the classroom newspaper, has recently sponsored national invention contests. More than 300,000 students entered the contests. Here are some of the contestants and their ideas—dramatic evidence that young people can think up amazing and useful inventions.*

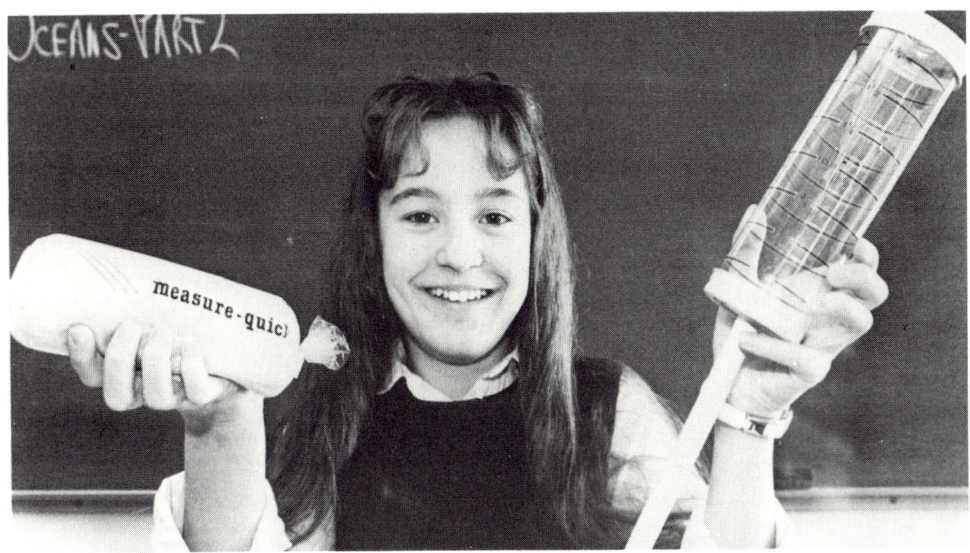

Sixth-grader Anna Thompson's **Measure Quick Shortening Dispenser** *makes a cook's job easier.*

First-grader Suzie Amling (right) won a grand prize for her **Line Leader and Keeper.** *Suzie's invention helps her teacher keep students in line as they walk along a busy street to the library. Suzie designed a rope with handles for each child. If a child lets go of a handle, a box at the teacher's end of the rope beeps a warning.*

ABOVE: *Katie Harding, a kindergartner, invented the* **Mudpuddle-Spotter**—*an umbrella with a flashlight attached to the handle. It helps her avoid puddles while walking along her driveway after dark.*

ABOVE RIGHT: *Kim Mehuron, a third-grader, invented the* **Jim Dandy Unlosable Toothpaste Cap** *to prevent the cap from going down the drain. The cap is permanently attached to the tube of toothpaste with a rubber band.*

LEFT: *Fifth-grader Chris Robben's baby brother chewed on the germ-ridden handles of shopping carts at the supermarket. So Chris cut a plastic shower-rod cover that fits over the shopping cart handle. He calls it the* **Germ Buster**. *Now his brother can chew to his heart's content and not get sick.*

RIGHT: *Jim Wollin, an eighth-grader, invented the clever* **Jar of Plenty** *to help people get to the bottom of food jars. Jim's jar has a lid at both ends, so reaching all the food in the jar is easy.*

BELOW: *Seventh-grader Clint Vaught won a grand prize for his* **Logg Hogg Lifting Arm**. *The invention helps Clint split heavy logs when his dad's not around. It lifts the logs onto a log splitter that cuts them into suitable sizes for the Vaughts' stove.*

Second-grader Ryan Johnson won a prize for his **Keep-Warm Bird Feeder**. Ryan's mom was cold when she went outside to feed the birds each morning, so Ryan came up with a way to do the job without leaving the house. He cut a small door in the wall of his home. The door opens into the outside bird feeder.

Kindergartner Daniel Randall solved the problem of dangling shoelaces with his **Shoe Magnet**. He thought of metal tips for shoelaces that cling to magnets on the shoes and keep the laces out of the way.

Fourth-grader Jennifer Acosta came up with a **Pop Top Mouthpiece**. Jennifer's reusable mouthpiece snaps into the slot where the top was pulled off a not-so-clean can and allows the user to drink without fear of germs.

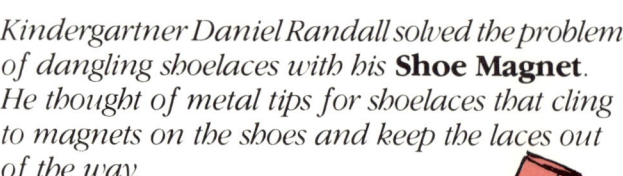

Suzanna Goodin, a first-grader, won a grand prize for creating the first **Edible Pet Food Server**. She got the idea for the invention because she was tired of washing spoons after she fed her kittens. The server is a cracker in the shape of a spoon that a pet can eat as part of its dinner after the "spoon" has been used to serve pet food.

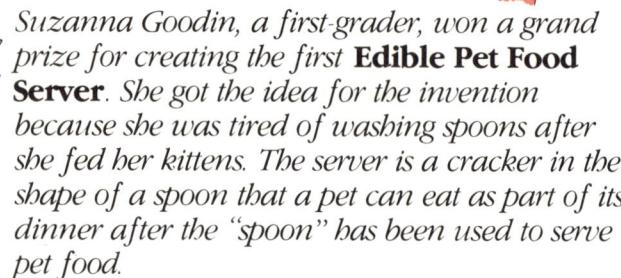

Jennifer Horowitz, a fifth-grader, sat at the corner of her dinner table where the table leg always got in her way. So Jenny invented the **Special Corner Chair**. It has a groove cut into the seat so that Jenny can pull right up to the table leg and straddle it.

Sixth-grader Scott Burnett invented his **School Bus Early Warning System** so he can wait for the school bus inside his home when the weather is bad. Scott's invention picks up a signal from the bus on an FM radio while he sits safe and dry inside.

Eighth-grader Danielle Dorsey invented the **Clutch Crutch Cap** to help a person on crutches walk safely over ice and snow. The cap fits over the end of a crutch. It has sharp spikes that crack through the ice and support the person securely.

Mark Mueller was tired of soggy cereal. So the fourth-grader invented the **Cereal Plate**—a bowl with an angled bottom that keeps the cereal and the milk separate until they are mixed together.

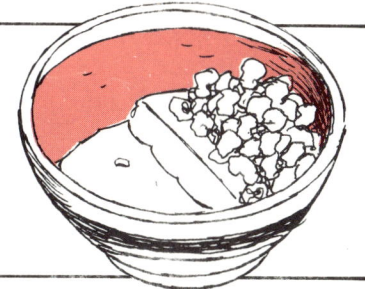

Third-grader April Baque's baby brother cried every time his mom used cold wipes at diaper-changing time. Now he's all smiles since April invented the **Baby Wipes Warmer**—a box that plugs into an electrical outlet to heat the wipes.

Second-grader Eric Vendura invented his **Sleeve Stopper** to help people put on coats without bunching up their sleeves. Eric's invention is a loop of elastic that is attached to each shirt or sweater sleeve. A person hooks a thumb into each loop before putting on his or her coat.

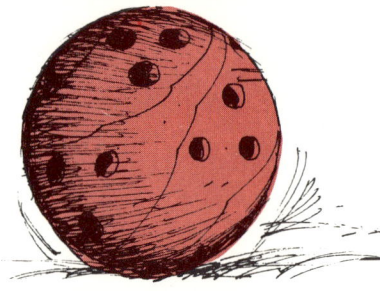

Third-grader Charlie Gurganus invented his **Bowling Ball** *to speed up a bowling game. Bowlers don't have to waste time looking for the finger holes because the ball is covered with them.*

Alex Nicander didn't have much use for his seesaw when his playmates weren't around. So the third-grader invented the **Seesaw Spring** *that fits under the empty seat. Now Alex can seesaw all by himself.*

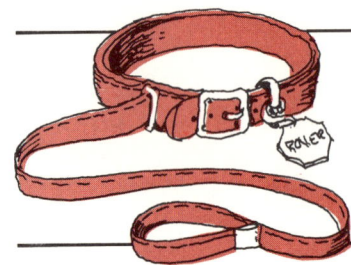

Fourth-grader Kristin Doherty invented the **Retractable Leash** *for her dog's collar. When it's walk time, Kristin doesn't search for the leash, she just pulls it out of the collar.*

Third-grader Kristine Adolph invented the **Super Toaster** *for forgetful people who burn their breakfast. Knife blades attached to the toaster pop out to scrape the sides of burned toast.*

Sixth-grader Aaron Snyder wanted to be in full control when pushing his wheelbarrow downhill. Now he is, because he invented the **Wheelbarrow Brake**.

CHAPTER 2
What Makes a Person "Inventive"?

When many people hear the word *inventor,* they picture a mad scientist with fuzzy hair surrounded by bubbling test tubes and generators crackling with electricity.

But, in fact, inventors are very much like the rest of us. They may be old or young, male or female, postgraduate students or kindergartners. They may work in multimillion-dollar laboratories or in family kitchens.

Yet inventors do have qualities in common that set them apart from other people. They are curious about the world around them. They have active imaginations. They are willing to work at solving problems. They have the confidence to make their inventions successful, regardless of what others think or say.

Let's take a closer look at some well-known inventors of the past and present to see what role these four factors played in their work.

INVENTORS ARE CURIOUS

Ever hear the saying "Necessity is the mother of invention"? If that's true, then curiosity might well be the father of invention. It is curiosity that sets the spark of creativity in the inventor's mind and starts him or her on the path to a new invention.

Think about Velcro®, the popular, lightweight, washable fastener that keeps your coat and book bag closed.

George de Mestral had just returned from a walk with his dog in the Swiss mountains near his home when he noticed his pet's fur was thick with burrs.

As de Mestral struggled to pull off the burrs, he wondered what made them cling so stubbornly to his dog. He looked at the burrs under a microscope and saw that they had tiny hooks that snagged onto the dog's fur. It suddenly occurred to de Mestral that if he could copy the hooks of the burr, he could invent the perfect fastener.

Touch fasteners, such as Velcro®, have many uses in a spacecraft. They can keep a notebook in place (upper right) and even hold an astronaut's lunch securely in place.

It wasn't until years later that the inventor got around to working on his fastener. After many experiments with different materials, de Mestral found a way to copy nature's hooks and loops and attach them to strips of cloth. In 1957 he patented his invention.

Today the Velcro fastener is used on everything from children's shoes to spacecraft supplies. It can withstand the heat of the tropics and the freezing cold of the Arctic. And we can thank a curious man out for a stroll for this popular product.

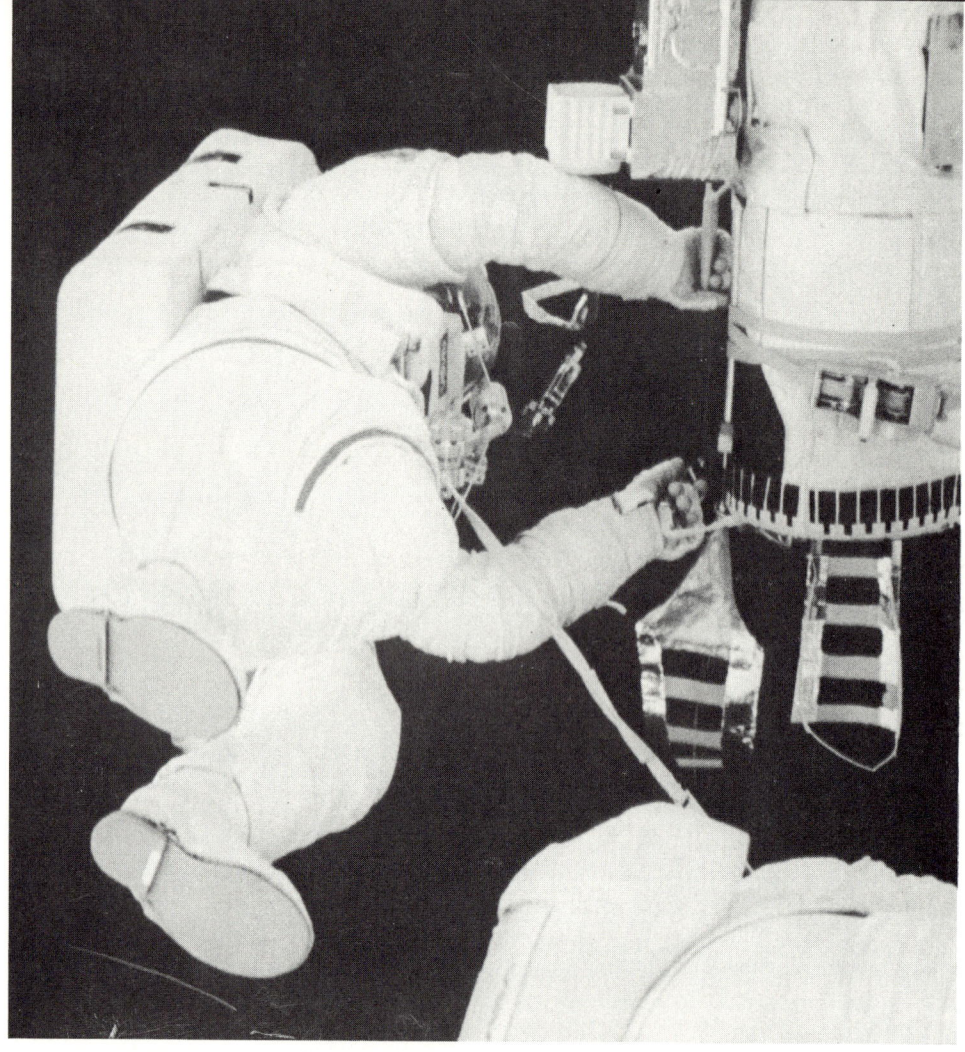

Theodore Marton's safety line enables an astronaut to move freely in space.

INVENTORS ARE IMAGINATIVE

It takes imagination to find the answer to a puzzling problem even though that answer may be right under the inventor's nose.

In 1960, scientist Theodore Marton was looking for a way to bring an astronaut in space back safely into a spacecraft. A safety line to do the job had to be both flexible and rigid. It had to be flexible so that the astronaut could move about freely in space. But it also had to be rigid to keep the weightless person from drifting about while being drawn back into the spacecraft.

Marton couldn't figure out how to make a line both rigid and flexible. Then one day, as he was watching his son play with a toy dog, he noticed something he hadn't really noticed before. When the boy pushed a button on the toy, the dog collapsed. Examining the toy, Marton saw that the dog was made of small segments and was kept erect by a tight string inside it. When the button was pushed, the string relaxed and the dog collapsed.

Marton used this idea in designing his safety line. The line is relaxed and flexible when an astronaut walks in space but it can be tightened, or made rigid, when the astronaut is towed back into the spacecraft. By using his imagination, Marton was able to apply the workings of a simple children's toy to create an important tool for space travel.

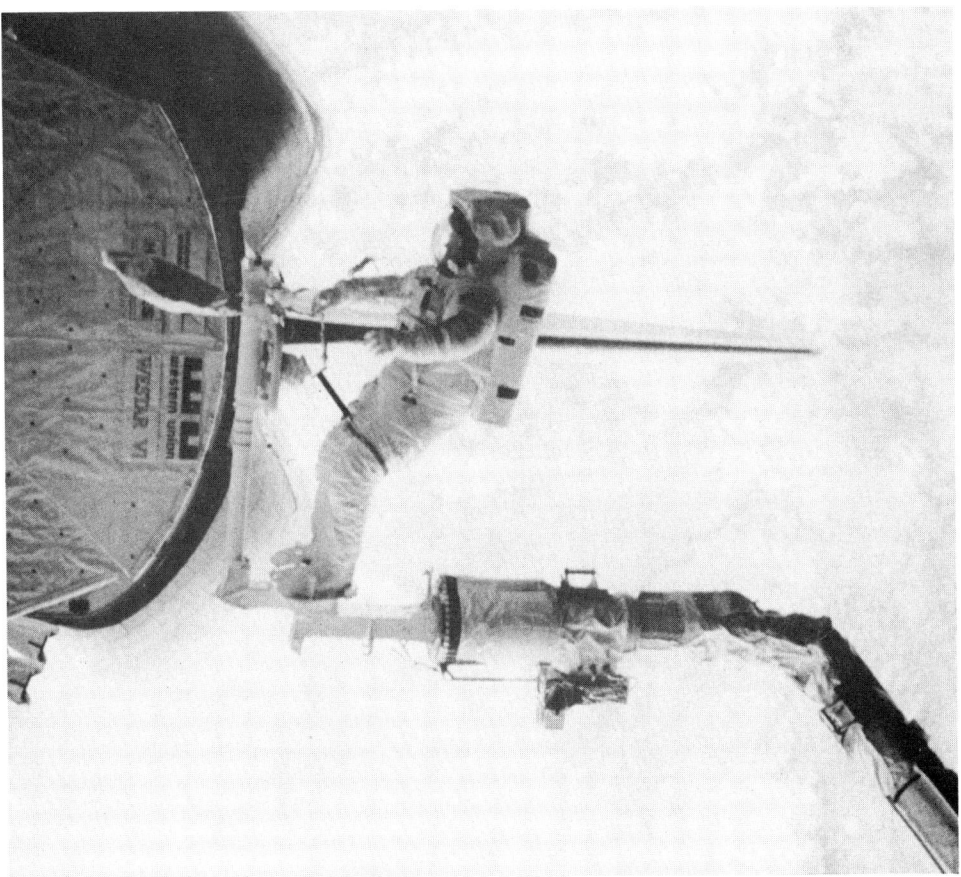

When an astronaut finishes his work in space, his safety line, made rigid, pulls him easily back into the spacecraft.

INVENTORS ARE PROBLEM SOLVERS

While working on a new invention, an inventor may face a number of different problems. The inventor's success or failure depends on how hard he or she is willing to work at solving these problems.

Jack St. Clair Kilby, an engineer working for Texas Instruments, is one inventor whose solution to a tough problem resulted in a revolution in the field of electronics.

Kilby's problem was parts—tens of thousands of them. In the mid-1950s, he and other electrical engineers were struggling to build an electric circuit. This circuit would have to perform the big jobs needed in the new electronic age of communications and space travel.

Jack S. Kilby, inventor of the first integrated circuit. Kilby refused to give up, and even worked on his research during his vacation. His persistence paid off. It was during the summer vacation of 1958 that Kilby completed his first great invention.

An electric circuit for such tasks had to hold hundreds of thousands of transistors, resistors, and capacitors. All these parts had to be connected in one unbroken path along which current could flow. To wire and solder all these parts together would be a nightmare. One mistake, and the path would be broken; current would not flow. And even if such a circuit could be designed, it would be so gigantic it could never fit in a newsroom or a rocket going to the moon.

Many engineers believed such a circuit could never be built, but Jack Kilby disagreed. He took fresh approaches to solving this difficult problem. One approach was to think in miniature. Why not put an entire electric circuit together on a single chip of silicon? The silicon would conduct electric charges to all parts of the circuit at once so there would be no need to wire or solder the parts. And the parts could be squeezed onto a space no larger than a fingernail.

In 1958 Kilby made his idea a reality. He built the first integrated circuit, or *chip*, as it came to be called. Today, the chip is the heart of every computer.

As computer chips developed, they got progressively smaller.

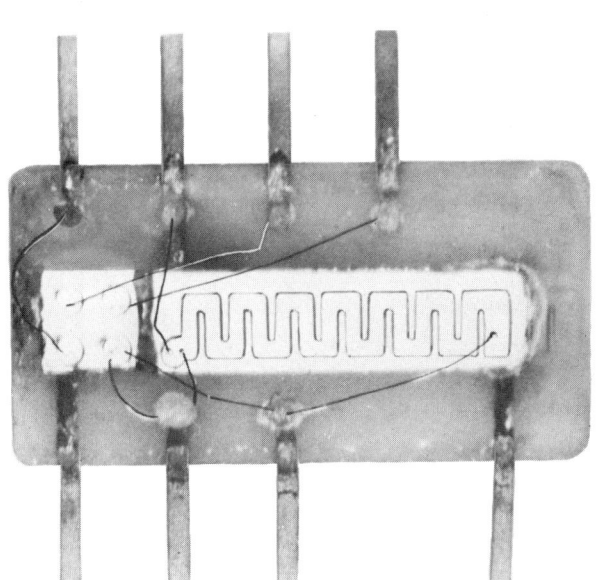

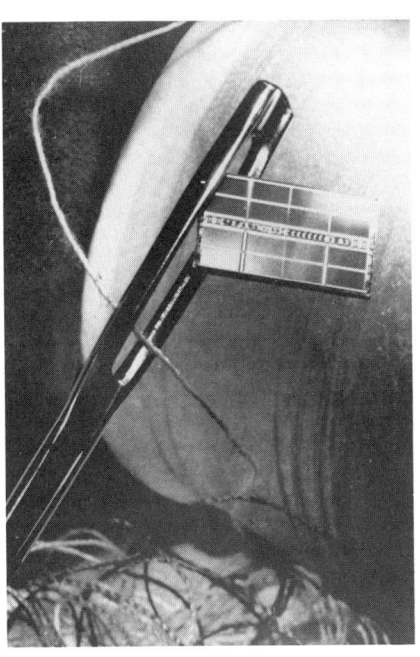

The first integrated circuit (above, left), invented by Jack Kilby. More recent chips not only are smaller than the original, but can store much more information. The chip shown on the right can store 1 million bits of information, yet is small enough to fit through the eye of a needle.

Elias Howe, inventor of the sewing machine

INVENTORS HAVE CONFIDENCE

Solving problems and creating an invention do not always guarantee success for an inventor. Many times the inventor must convince the rest of the world that his or her invention is useful.

Few have needed confidence more than Elias Howe, the inventor of the sewing machine. In the long years it took to find acceptance for his great invention, Howe lost nearly everything he had.

It all started one fateful day in 1841. Twenty-two-year-old Howe was working in a Boston machine shop when he overheard his boss talking to an inventor friend.

"If you can invent a sewing machine that would replace sewing by hand, it would make you a fortune," said Howe's boss.

We don't know if the friend ever took the advice, but young Howe was inspired by it. He decided then and there to invent a machine that could sew. But his fortune was a long time in coming.

For five years he worked at making a sewing machine. His family had little money to live on and, ironically, Howe's wife had to take in sewing to help support her husband.

Finally, Howe finished making a workable sewing machine. But the tailors of Boston laughed when they heard of it. They said a machine could never match the quality of their handwork. The inventor surprised them all, however, when he held a contest between his sewing machine and five of the fastest seamstresses in the city. The sewing machine, operated by Howe, won easily, finishing the sewing in a quarter of the time it took the seamstresses.

Unfortunately, Howe's machine, although fast, was very expensive to produce. There wasn't a manufacturer in America who would touch it, so Howe went to England. There, a manufacturer of umbrellas and leather bags bought his invention. It seemed that Howe's fortune was

The 1870 Howe sewing machine featured Howe's patented lock stitch.

about to be made. But the English manufacturer wanted to make women's undergarments with the sewing machine. Howe protested that his invention was not ready for this kind of sewing. Then he complained about the small amount of money he was getting from the manufacturer, and, finally, quit and withdrew his invention. Penniless and unable to feed his family, Howe decided to return to America. While his wife and children traveled in one ship across the Atlantic, Howe had to work his way back on another ship—as a cook.

Just when things looked blackest for Elias Howe, America began to take an interest in the sewing machine. But other men were making money with Howe's invention without his permission, so Howe borrowed every penny he could and took the manufacturers to court. The long legal battle that followed was known by newspaper readers everywhere as the "sewing machine war." Finally, Howe was declared the victor in this "war" and the courts awarded him a royalty of five dollars for every sewing machine made and sold by other manufacturers. That was a considerable payment in those days. At last successful and rich, Howe never forgot the long years of struggle. He gave generously to the poor and needy until the day he died.

Curiosity, imagination, willingness to work at solving problems, and confidence—these are the qualities that make an inventive person and, more than that, a successful inventor.

CHAPTER 3
Strange and Unusual Inventions

Some inventions are so much a part of our lives that we cannot imagine being without them. Think what your life would be like without light bulbs, television, or telephones.

On the other hand, some inventions have very particular and special uses. You might consider many of these inventions strange, but the United States government grants their inventors protection, called a patent, because the inventions are new and different, and because some people might find them useful.

Here are five unusual patented products. See if you can guess their uses. Then check the description of each invention on page 74.

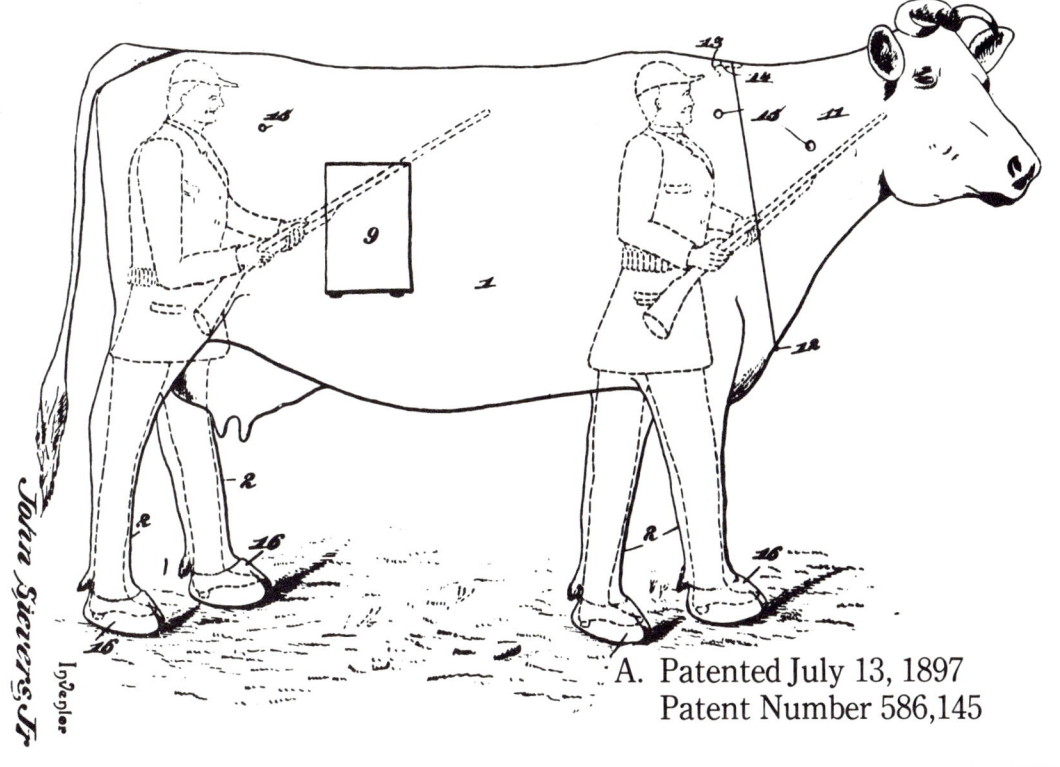

A. Patented July 13, 1897
Patent Number 586,145

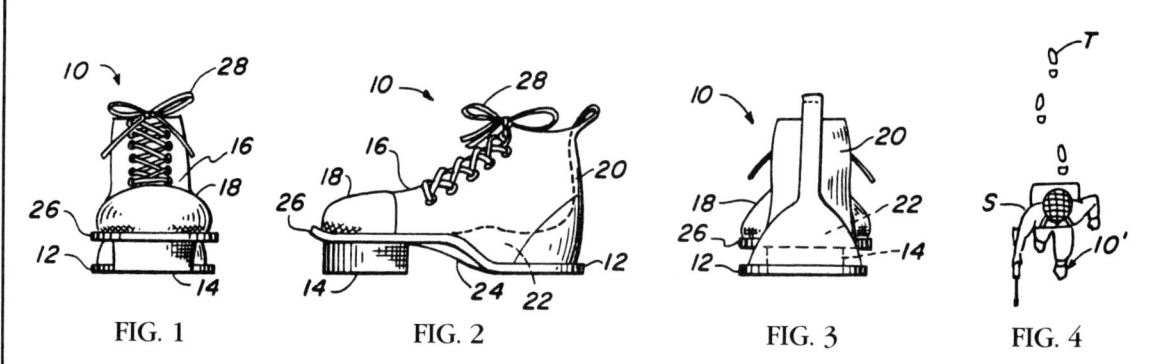

B. Patented July 16, 1974
   Patent Number 3,823,494

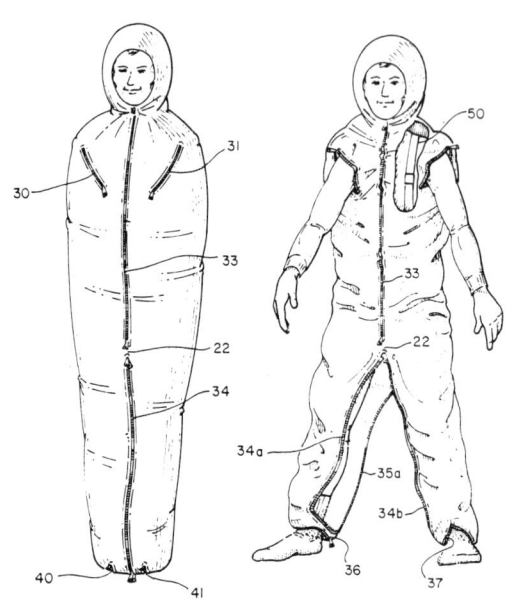

C. Patented April 2, 1985
   Patent Number 4,507,805

D. Patented November 18, 1879
   Patent Number 221,855

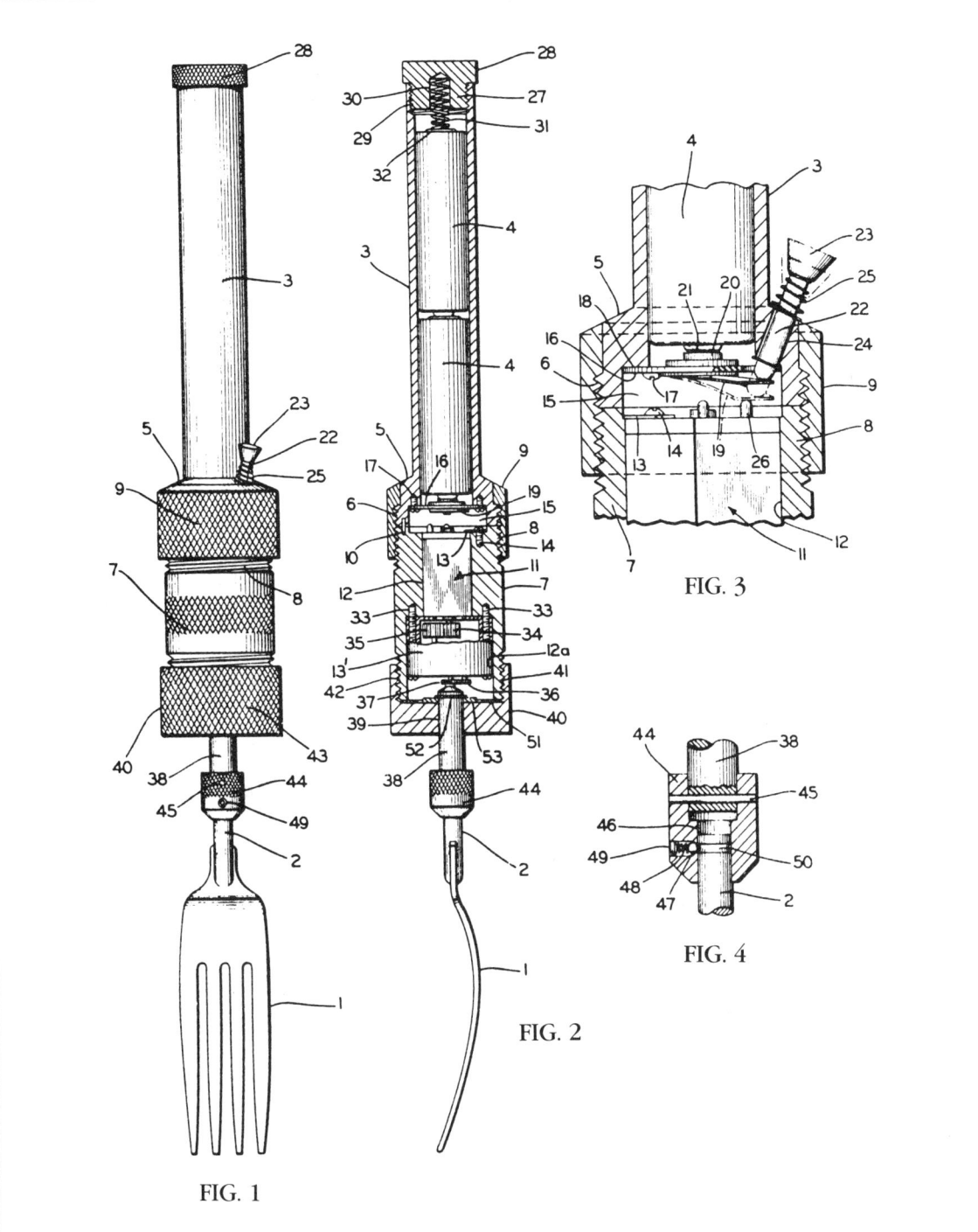

FIG. 1

FIG. 2

FIG. 3

FIG. 4

E. Patented June 29, 1971
Patent Number 3,589,009

CHAPTER 4
A Behind-the-Scenes Look at Some Inventions

Have you ever asked yourself, "Why didn't I think of that?" when you've seen an invention you liked?

Why does one person think of the idea for an invention before anyone else does? Let's take a behind-the-scenes look at how some inventions came to be. There may be lessons to learn from these stories.

SOMETHING TO KEEP THE EARS WARM

Some inventors invent things that they themselves need. Then they discover, often to their surprise, that other people need their invention, too.

Fifteen-year-old Chester Greenwood of Farmington, Maine, had a problem with his ears. They were very sensitive to the freezing cold of the long Maine winters.

While other children his age would race sleds down slopes, build ice forts, and skate on frozen ponds, poor Chester would rub his ears and go home.

One December day in 1873, Chester decided he had to do something. He tied a scarf around his head, but it itched and would not stay in place. Then he hit upon the idea of covering just his ears. Chester bent a piece of wire into loops, fitted the loops over his ears, and attached the loops to a hat. Chester asked his grandmother to cover them with wool and fur.

These early ads show the inventor of earmuffs proudly promoting his product. Chester Greenwood's imagination served him well all of his life. He is credited with more than 100 other inventions.

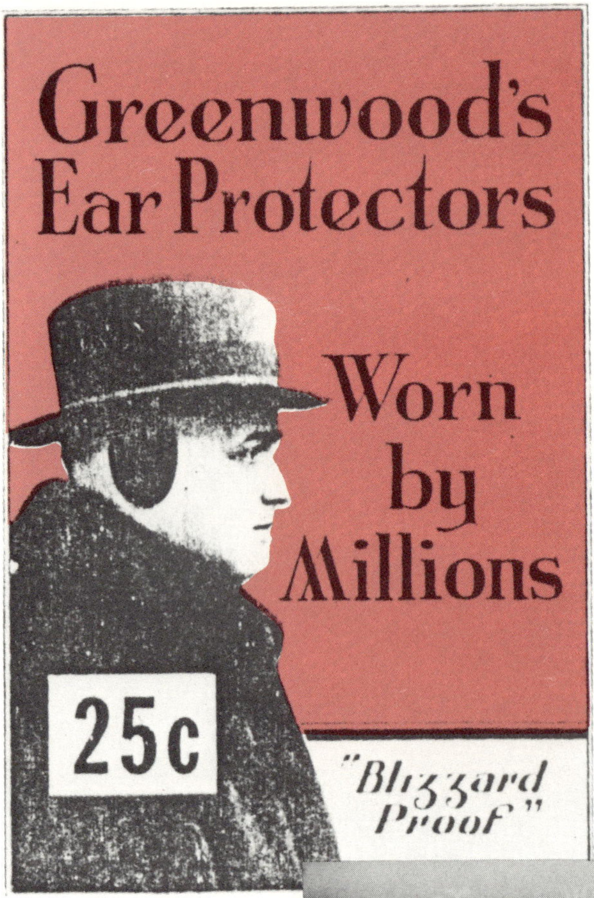

When the other kids saw Chester in his strange headgear, they laughed. But the laughter stopped when they realized that Chester was staying outside in the cold longer than he ever had before. Soon the other kids were asking Chester if he would make them covers for their ears. Chester Greenwood realized he was on to something big.

Orders from all over town started pouring in. Chester's mom and grandmother were busy helping him make more earmuffs, the name people were calling Greenwood's clever invention.

As word of Chester's earmuffs spread throughout New England, the inventor found ways to improve his invention. Instead of attaching the ear covers to a hat, Chester fastened them to the end of a strip of flat metal that he fitted over his head. The band held the ear covers firmly in place.

By the time he was 19, Chester had received a patent for his invention and was well on his way to becoming rich and successful. To keep up with all the orders, he designed machines to manufacture the earmuffs, and set up a factory right in Farmington. Although he went on to produce many other inventions, Chester continued to operate his earmuff factory until his death in 1937.

Today Farmington, Maine, is known as "the earmuff capital of the world." Every year on December 21, the first day of winter, Farmington celebrates "Chester Greenwood Day" to honor a clever boy who found a way to keep his ears—and millions of other ears—warm.

HERO OF THE SAFETY HOOD

Some people create inventions that make life safer for others. They get their ideas by thinking of other people's welfare instead of their own needs or comforts.

Garrett Morgan, pioneer in safety

Garrett Morgan was granted a patent in 1912 for the Morgan Safety Hood, a special breathing helmet that pumped air directly into a mask that fitted over a person's face. The air was stored in a bag attached to the mask. There was enough air in the bag for 15 to 20 minutes of breathing—enough time for a firefighter to enter a smoke-filled burning building and rescue people inside.

Morgan was awarded the grand prize at the Industrial Exposition of Safety in New York in 1914, but it wasn't until an unexpected disaster in 1916 that Morgan and his invention became famous.

One night a tunnel collapsed 250 feet below the surface of Lake Erie in Morgan's hometown of Cleveland, Ohio. Workers from the Cleveland Waterworks were overcome by deadly gas fumes and trapped in the tunnel. Poisonous gas drove back firefighters who tried to reach the trapped men. But someone at the scene of the disaster remembered seeing Morgan give a demonstration of his safety hood some weeks before.

Police quickly located the inventor and asked him to come to their aid. Morgan, accompanied by his brother, arrived at the scene of the disaster with safety hoods. The two entered the clouded tunnel to rescue the helpless workers inside.

Morgan and his brother succeeded in carrying all 32 trapped workmen from the tunnel. Fortunately, many were still alive and the inventor was proclaimed a hero. As news spread of the daring rescue, his safety hood became a great success. Soon it was standard equipment in fire departments across the nation.

When the United States entered World War I, Morgan adapted his safety hood into a gas mask that was worn by American soldiers fighting in Europe. The masks protected them from deadly chlorine fumes on the battlefield.

Garrett Morgan continued to invent, keeping other people's welfare in mind. He designed the first three-way traffic signal, making roadways safer for millions of motorists. Before he died in 1963 at the age of 86, Garrett Morgan had lived to see the United States a safer country, thanks to his inventions.

U.S. soldiers during World War I wore gas masks to protect them from deadly chlorine fumes.

Frisbee enthusiasts celebrate at the annual National Frisbee Festival.

THE FABULOUS FRISBEE

Some inventors take a common item already in existence and find an entirely new use for it. That's how the popular toy the Frisbee came to be.

One day in 1948, Walter Fred Morrison happened to be driving past the Frisbie Pie Company in Bridgeport, Connecticut, when he saw two truck drivers tossing empty pie pans back and forth in the parking lot.

It reminded Morrison of his childhood, when he'd thrown pie pans with his playmates. Returning home to Los Angeles, California, Morrison went to work designing a disc that could be thrown back and forth like the pie pans. The disc

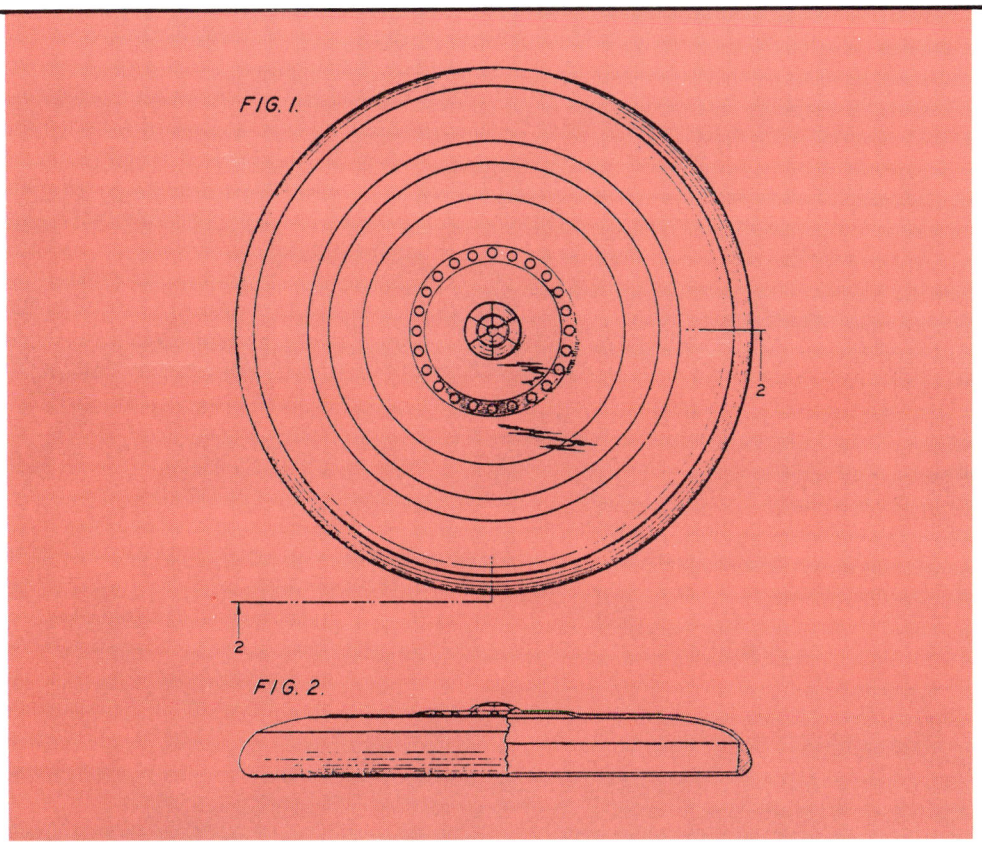

The drawing that Walker Morrison submitted with his 1957 patent application for a "Flying Toy"

had to be light enough not to hurt someone who got in its flight path and still heavy enough to fly a good distance. He found the right material for his toy—a soft plastic that was bouncy but tough. He called his invention "Morrison's Flyin' Saucer" and took two cartons of his toys to a nearby county fair to sell.

Morrison thought of a gimmick to make people want to buy his flying saucers. He told the crowds at the fair that there was an "invisible wire" stretched between him and a friend. When Morrison threw the saucer, he claimed it flew along the wire directly to his friend's waiting hand. Morrison charged one cent per foot for the invisible wire and threw in a "free" Flyin' Saucer with every 100 feet of wire a customer bought. The gimmick worked and soon Morrison had sold out his supply of saucers and invisible wire.

But Morrison still wasn't satisfied. He improved the design and gave the toy a new name—the Pluto Platter. In 1957, the Wham-O Toy Company of San Gabriel, California, saw the Pluto Platter, liked it, and bought it from Morrison.

Sales of Pluto Platters were steady among beachgoers who loved playing catch with them, but were slow among the general public. Then one day, Wham-O owner Rich Knerr saw some college students throwing the Platters at Harvard University in Cambridge, Massachusetts. The students told him how they used to throw pie pans from the Frisbie Pie Company. Knerr remembered Morrison's story about the same pie company and decided that a change of name would make the toy more popular. The Pluto Platter became the Frisbee (an unintentional misspelling) and the rest is history.

The Frisbee remains popular with people of all ages and athletic abilities. And it all started with an empty pie pan and an inventor with imagination.

Even dogs get into the action! Canine Frisbee star, Lady, performs in the Doggie Catch and Fetch Frisbee Contest. Her master (right) is just as enthusiastic.

FROM CHICLE TO CHEWING GUM

What is worthless to one person may be valuable to someone else. And when that someone else happens to be an inventor, the results can be spectacular.

Take the case of Thomas Adams of New Jersey. Adams turned a supply of apparently useless tree sap sitting in his warehouse into a new product—chewing gum.

The dried sap Adams had is called *chicle*. It comes from the wild sapodilla tree of Central America. Adams had spent two years trying to make a substitute for rubber from the chicle but his efforts had failed. Then Adams noticed his young son chewing chicle in imitation of the Indians who had chewed it for over a thousand years. What was good for the Indians, thought Adams, might just be enjoyable to the folks at home. At that time, Americans were chewing less tasty materials such as spruce resin and paraffin.

The makers of Black Jack gum cashed in on its popularity by running a contest in 1927. The gum has proved so popular you can still buy it today.

So Adams and his sons, Horatio and Thomas, went to work. They mixed chicle with water, rolled it into balls, and sold it to druggists along the East Coast. Customers welcomed the flavorless chewing gum and, by 1872, Adams was operating his own chewing-gum factory with 250 workers.

Despite teachers who outlawed it in schools and doctors who mistakenly warned that it would make the intestines stick together if swallowed, chewing gum became a worldwide success.

Adams constantly improved his product. He changed the packaging, sold it in vending machines, and added numerous flavors. You can still buy his licorice-flavored Black Jack in stores today.

SOAP THAT FLOATS

An invention can sometimes happen by accident.

You've probably seen a movie where a great inventor suddenly discovers his invention as the result of a complete accident. It might seem corny, but once in a while this is exactly what happens to real inventors.

Of course, the inventor must be able to find out how the accident happened, make it happen again, and turn it into something meaningful.

Art from an early ad for Ivory Soap

Just such an accident happened at the Procter and Gamble soap company in 1879. A worker left for lunch and forgot to turn off the soap mixer. More than the usual amount of air was whipped into a batch of the pure white soap that the company made and sold under the name The White Soap.

Too embarrassed to tell his boss about the mistake, the worker kept it a secret. The air-filled soap was packaged and shipped to customers around the country. Before long, customers were writing to Procter and Gamble asking for more of the "soap that floats." People liked the soap because they never had to hunt at the bottom of the tub for it. Company officials knew a good thing when they saw it. After investigating the accident and finding what had caused it, they turned it into one of their most successful products—Ivory Soap. For many years, it was advertised as the soap that floats.

And what happened to the accidental inventor who made the lucky mistake? We don't know, but he should have been given a bonus for being so forgetful!

IVORY SOAP

Purity

IVORY SOAP. [IVORY] **.99 44/100 % PURE**

IT FLOATS

The accident that paid off: For many years, Ivory Soap was advertised as the soap that floats.

Rebecca Schroeder uses her glow sheet.

GLOW, LITTLE GLOW SHEET

Some inventors adapt their inventions to meet the needs of others.

Rebecca Schroeder was only nine when she invented the glow sheet. She went for a drive with her mother and sat in the car doing homework while her mother went shopping. Soon it began to grow dark and Rebecca could no longer see well enough to write. As the light grew dimmer, another kind of light lit up in Rebecca's brain. Why not make a board or panel, she thought, that would light up so that people could write in the dark?

It was a great idea, but how was she going to turn it into a practical invention? Rebecca asked her father, a patent attorney and an inventor himself, to buy her some luminous paint. Then one night, after experimenting with the paint in her bedroom, she came running out to tell her surprised parents, "It works! It works!"

Rebecca's invention, which she calls the "Glow Sheet," consists of a sheet of special luminous paper embedded in a plastic clipboard. When a sheet of writing paper is placed over the clipboard, it lights up. The darker it is, the brighter the paper glows. When she found that the glow sheet began to lose its glow after 15 minutes, Rebecca found a way to lengthen the glow's life. She wired the clipboard with electricity and attached a battery-operated button. To "turn" the glow sheet on, a person only had to push the button.

Today, in her mid-20s, Rebecca heads her own company, BJ Products. (BJ stands for Becky Jane.) She works at trying to get her glow sheets produced as inexpensively as possible so that many people will be able to afford to buy them.

And she's busy promoting her glow sheet idea to various groups and individuals. She is always thinking up new ways to make her invention useful. For example, with the glow sheet, hospital nurses could write their reports without turning on the lights and disturbing a sleeping patient. Police officers could fill out reports in emergencies or at the darkened scene of a crime.

Rebecca worked diligently at creating and improving her invention.

Radiologists and photographers, who must develop their X rays and photographs in darkened rooms, could take notes without damaging their work. And customers in dimly lit restaurants could read the menu more easily.

Finally, Rebecca's invention could help other inventors. When an idea for a new invention comes in the middle of the night, an inventor could just reach for the glow sheet on the bedside table and jot down the idea. In the morning, the inventor would be ready to start working on that midnight inspiration!

CHAPTER 5
Getting Started

If you're inspired by the example of other inventors and you think you have what it takes to join their ranks, how do you get started?

Every invention begins with an idea. But where does the all-important idea come from? It comes from you or the people you know.

ASK AROUND

Every successful invention fulfills a need. Sometimes it's a personal need, sometimes it's a need shared by many people. You know what you need. The way to find out about the needs of others is to ask questions. Talk to your friends, neighbors, classmates, and family members. Ask them what would make their jobs easier or their lives more fun.

Clarence Birdseye, a member of a U.S. government survey team in Labrador in 1915, asked the local people what they needed most. The answer he got was fresh foods. Few vegetables or meats could be produced in such a cold, northern land and there was no way to transport foods there without spoilage.

Frozen foods had been available commercially in the United

Clarence Birdseye, shown dictating in his office in 1943. Surveying his customers regularly, the inventor never stopped trying to make his products better.

Birds Eye® frozen food from early times (far right) to modern (left).

States since 1865, but they had little flavor when they were thawed. Birdseye noticed that fish frozen very quickly by the Labradorean natives retained all its flavor after being thawed. It occurred to him that the problem with commercial freezing was that it was done too slowly. The food spoiled partially during the long freezing process and food cells were damaged.

After several years of experimenting, Birdseye developed a process to quick-freeze foods and came to be known as the "Father of Frozen Foods."

But Clarence Birdseye never stopped asking questions. He surveyed his customers regularly to see what new kinds of frozen foods they wanted. Today you can still buy Birds Eye® frozen foods, named after the inventor of modern quick-freezing.

Birdseye did not only ask questions; he set out to improve something that already existed—frozen foods. Not every invention needs to be new. There's always room for taking an old idea and making it better.

Inventor's Question Box

GETTING AN IDEA

- What products do I or my friends use that could work better? Be more appealing? Be made to do more? Be made for less?
- Is there something that would make a person's job easier?
- What particular problem would I like solved?

CHECKING AN IDEA

- Is this idea really new? Is it practical?
- Will enough people want this invention to make it profitable?
- Can this invention be made at a reasonable cost?

Marconi at his receiving set in Newfoundland on December 12, 1901. The date marked history's first transatlantic wireless transmission.

GET THE FACTS

Inventors need more than original ideas to develop an invention. They need to learn everything they can about the subject areas related to their ideas. This information helps them plan, design, and refine their inventions. Clarence Birdseye had to learn all about ice crystals before he could successfully freeze food. Marconi took physics courses to find out how sound travels. George Eastman learned about chemicals and early photography before he invented film and the Kodak camera. And Melville Bissell, inventor of the carpet sweeper, had to become an expert on a subject as simple as brushes to help him with his famous invention.

You, too, will need to become an expert on your subject. Read all you can about it—in books, magazines, and journals—and add constantly to your collection of information. If possible, contact manufacturers and organizations specializing in your subject.

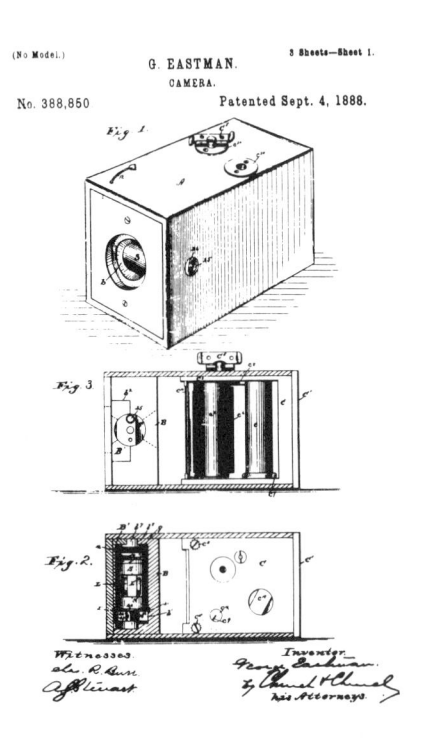

The drawing (left) that accompanied George Eastman's camera patent application. Eastman (right), the inventor, held two jobs in his early days of inventing: Bank clerk by day, inventor by night. Years of study and work went into his invention of film and the first Kodak camera (below).

Melville Bissell (left), inventor of the carpet sweeper. An early popular model of his invention (right). The first Bissell carpet sweeper (below) came about when the inventor, allergic to dust, tried to figure out a way to get rid of the dust in his shop.

Inventor's Question Box

GETTING THE FACTS

- What subject areas should I read about and study before going ahead with my invention?

- What specific information will I need to know to make my invention work?

- What books or periodicals might add to my knowledge of my subject?

- What persons or organizations might be of help?

Gail Borden

TAKE YOUR TIME

You've probably heard the old saying "Rome wasn't built in a day." The same could be said for a successful invention. Asking questions, researching facts, and thinking your invention through in every detail all take time. If you rush past any step, you may overlook something important.

Gail Borden spent years inventing a way to preserve milk. In the 1800s, there was no refrigeration, and milk often went bad before consumers drank it. Many people became sick drinking this contaminated milk; some even died.

Borden believed that if he could remove the water from milk—condense it—it could be canned and remain safe for long periods of time. He tested and retested many methods for condensing. He checked and rechecked each step in his process. But when he succeeded and applied for a patent on his condensing method, the U.S. Patent Office turned him down. They claimed his process showed "nothing new."

But Gail Borden did not give up. He kept working at his invention. Finally, in 1856, he proved his condensing method new and workable and was granted a patent.

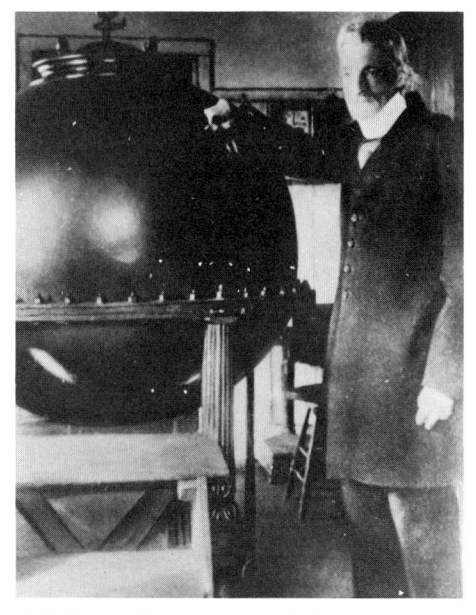

A helper who witnessed the event stands by the device that Gail Borden used in his first successful experiment to condense milk.

He was soon operating the world's first condensed-milk factory. Today the Borden Company still turns out millions of cans of condensed milk, as well as many other dairy products, for people everywhere.

Borden had a saying that was later engraved on his tombstone, words that every inventor should keep in mind, especially when things are going wrong: *I tried and failed; I tried again and again, and succeeded.*

Gail Borden first began to sell his condensed milk from this pushcart in New York City.

Inventor's Question Box
TAKING YOUR TIME

- How can I test my invention to make sure it works?

- Have I overlooked anything in designing my invention?

- What questions will someone else have about my invention?

KEEP A NOTEBOOK

Before you go to work on your invention, get a notebook and keep it handy. Inventors say their notebooks are their most valuable tools. They fill them with notes on their ideas and the materials they use, test results, progress reports, and things they learn while working on their inventions.

As you fill up your notebook, get witnesses—friends or family members—to sign some dated entries. This is valuable proof that your invention is your idea and no one else's. You might need to present these witnessed records to the U.S. Patent Office if someone else claims to have invented the same invention before you did.

Alexander Graham Bell in 1876, the year the telephone was patented

An artist's conception of the first successful use of the telephone. An excited assistant rushes in to tell Bell that he has just heard Bell's voice distinctly over the transmitter.

Daniel Drawbaugh learned this lesson the hard way. If he had kept a notebook containing witnesses' signatures, he might today be honored as the inventor of the telephone. Witnesses claimed they had heard him talk over his telephone long before Alexander Graham Bell even filed a patent application for the same invention in 1876. But their words weren't good enough in a court of law. The law wanted written, dated testimony and that was the one thing Drawbaugh couldn't produce.

Bell's first telephone

An ad for Thomas A. Edison's phonograph (left). In another advertising campaign, opera singer Alice Verlet (right) sang beside the phonograph, challenging listeners to distinguish between her real and recorded voices.

The original phonograph patented by Edison in 1828

To avoid cases like Drawbaugh's, patent officials stress the importance to inventors of notebooks to show when their work on an invention began and how they followed through on the idea.

Thomas Edison, inventor of the phonograph, the electric lamp, and the kinetoscope, among other things, called the work he did in his notebooks "thinking on paper." He filled hundreds of notebooks and sketchbooks with notes, diagrams, and drawings. For the electric lamp alone, he wrote more than 40,000 pages of notes!

After months of experiments, Edison invented the first practical electric incandescent lamp (above). Edison, holding one of his lamps (left), dedicated his life to inventing, and was willing to do the necessary work. "Invention is 1 percent inspiration and 99 percent perspiration," he said. He went on to patent 1,093 inventions during his lifetime.

Edison and his home projecting kinetoscope

You, too, will come to value your notebooks.
These written records of your invention's progress will help you plan, think through your ideas, and solve problems. You will want to share them with experts and fellow inventors.

Here are sample pages from an inventor's notebook. Use them as a guide to start a notebook of your own.

MY INVENTION NOTEBOOK

Date _Spring and Summer, 1972_

Invention idea _window screens for car window_

Title of invention _Bug Guard. Auto Screen. Clear Breeze._

Product will be used by _drivers who can't afford air conditioning, parents of little kids_

Number of users _All car owners_

Material needed   Cost (approximate)

screen (one window) $2.00
framing $1.75
fasteners, latches, snaps $2.25

Collecting Information

Questions asked _Do you have air conditioning? Do you have trouble with bugs? Would you use a window screen?_

People asked/Remarks _____ Date _____

A. _Mother — April 12. great idea — I need it, cost not important._

B. <u>younger brother – April 14. Can I put my hand out the window?</u>
C. <u>neighbor Mr. Lee – Is it easy to install?</u>
D. <u>Grandpa – May 6. Would it cost much?</u>

Product Research

Question <u>Are there screens for car windows?</u>

Date <u>May 8</u>
Source <u>Auto Supply Store</u>
Answer <u>not in store / not in catalog</u> Peter Messier, Manager, ABC Auto Supply 5/8/72

Question <u>Could screen be installed by owner?</u>

Date <u>May 10</u>
Source <u>family</u>
Answer <u>Mom put up my model on driver's window easily. It came down easily, no marks on car.</u>

Tests

Test #1 <u>vision OK?</u>

Date <u>May 10</u>
Results 1 <u>Dad could see fine, better with fine screen, gray color</u>
Test #2 <u>time to install (asked 4 people)</u>
Date <u>May 12</u>
Results 2 <u>four people, within 3 minutes for all</u>

CHAPTER 6
Thinking Like An Inventor

Take a tip from a winning baseball pitcher—warm up before you go to work. The pitcher warms up his pitching arm. As an inventor, you need to warm up your thinking skills. The brain-stretching problems in this chapter will help you do just that.

Inventors use some specific thinking skills. The exercises that end each section of this chapter will give you practice in thinking like an inventor to find new ideas and to solve problems.

BRAINSTORMING

"I just had a brainstorm!"

Did you ever hear somebody say this? It means he or she has come up with a very good, original idea. Most people think brainstorms just "happen." *But you can learn to brainstorm.*

Brainstorming is a great way to get ideas for inventions or to solve a problem. Here's how to go about it:

- Think of as many ideas as you can—*fast*. The more ideas you come up with, the better. List *all* your ideas, even the wild ones. You never know which one might be the inspiration for a new invention.
- When ideas stop coming (usually in about 20 minutes), stop and read over your list.
- Underline the best ideas.
- Test them out for workability and practicality.

You can brainstorm by yourself or with friends. Inventors say that hearing the ideas of others often sparks more ideas of their own.

INSTANT EXERCISES

1. Use the list below to practice brainstorming. Come up with as many unusual uses for each thing as you can.
   - a paper clip
   - a balloon
   - a paper bag
   - a jar with a lid
   - a shoelace
   - a rubber band

2. Use the list of problems below to practice brainstorming for solutions. Come up with as many different solutions to each problem as you can.
   - keep an egg from breaking during a space launch
   - find an invisible person
   - contact home from a foreign city without using a telephone or postal service
   - apply paint to a ball
   - heat a meal in a lifeboat
   - warn a person on a distant mountaintop of danger

Now use your brainstorming skills to solve a problem of your own.

FINDING ALTERNATIVES

Like all good inventors, Gillette did not settle for just one or two solutions to a problem. He knew that many alternatives must be considered before the best solution is found.

In the late 1800s, King Gillette was an inventor in search of an invention. An ambitious salesman, Gillette longed to invent a product that people would use once, throw away, and then have to replace—and, of course, he would be the one to sell them the replacement.

King Gillette, the "king" of shaving

One morning, Gillette went into the bathroom to shave and discovered his straight razor was so dull he'd have to take it to a barber to have it sharpened. It suddenly occurred to Gillette that if he could invent a disposable, thin-edged blade, he could make the cumbersome, straight-edged razor obsolete, solve the shaving problems of the world, and have his throw-away product.

He ran out to the nearest hardware store and bought some pieces of brass, a small hand vise, files, and some steel ribbons used in clock springs. From this odd assortment of materials, he fashioned the first modern safety razor.

But before Gillette could start counting his millions, he had another major problem to solve—finding a thin yet strong material for his disposable razor blade. Gillette spent six years experimenting with different metals and materials before he found the right alternative—sheet steel.

With his designer and partner, William Nickerson, Gillette opened his first office about 1901 above a Boston fish shop. Another seven years went by before Gillette's safety razor was accepted by American men, who clung stubbornly to the old-fashioned straight razor. But once the public did accept his new razor, Gillette became the "king" of shaving.

An early ad for the Gillette Safety Razor featured sports personalities of the day.

INSTANT EXERCISES

1. Get into the habit of looking at things in different ways. Use the figure below to practice finding alternatives.

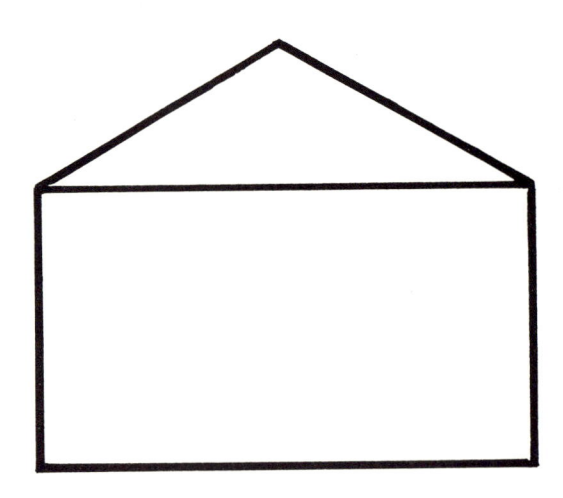

   What is it? It could be a triangle sitting on top of a rectangle. Or a house without a chimney. Or an envelope. List as many different answers to the question *what is it?* as you can. Then share your list with a friend and see if he or she can come up with some other alternatives.

2. Generate alternatives by asking yourself questions beginning with the two words *what if?* Read the question and problems to think about below. Then brainstorm as many alternatives as you can before settling on a solution to the problem.

   Question: What if chalkboards disappeared from schools?

   Problems to think about:
   - Where would students go for information?
   - What would teachers use instead to teach students?
   - How could we use chalk and erasers?

3. As you invent, practice going beyond the first idea that comes into your head. Try alternative solutions. You'll find yourself discovering new answers to your questions that never occurred to you before.

BLOCKBUSTING

When inventors find they are stuck on a problem, they often break their pattern of thinking by *blockbusting*. Following an entirely different train of thought, they often get new and different solutions to problems. They force themselves to think in unusual ways. For instance, they might think smaller or larger or in opposites or like someone living in another environment.

INSTANT EXERCISES

Practice breaking your thinking patterns with these brainteasers.

A. Take 12 pencils (or sticks, toothpicks, or strips of paper) and make four attached squares as shown. Change the four squares to seven squares by moving only two pencils.

   Hint: Think small.

B. Make the equation correct by moving only one pencil to another place in the equation.

   Hint: There are several solutions to this problem.

C. Turn the three pencils into four by moving only one pencil to another position. Breaking a pencil is not allowed.

   Hint: Think the way an ancient Roman would.

D. Change the pattern from five squares to four squares by moving only two pencils to other positions. You cannot double the pencils or place two pencils side by side.

   Hint: You can eliminate a whole square by moving only one pencil.

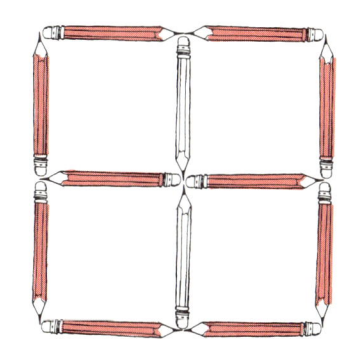

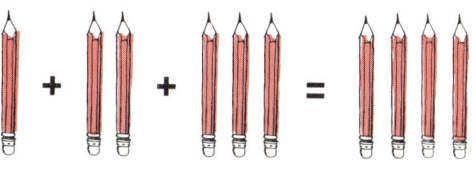

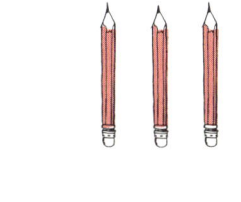

Answers to brainteasers are given on page 74.

MAKING ASSOCIATIONS

Inventors often get new ideas by making new associations with the things they observe around them. Some inventors, for instance, turn to the natural world for their inspiration. You read earlier how burrs inspired George de Mestral to invent a new fastener. But did you know that tree leaves were the basis for a new kind of potato chip?

Managers at a potato-chip company were looking for a way to pack their chips compactly without crushing them. One employee, watching leaves falling from a tree, realized that dry leaves crumble but wet leaves do not. He thought potato slices were like leaves. He tried stacking wet potato chips in containers and then drying the chips. The chips, like the wet leaves, did not crumble and could be packed one on top of another. A new chip was born: Pringles.

You too can use the world of nature as a springboard for a new invention. Take a nature walk. Find something that interests you—a plant, an inanimate object, even an animal. If you can, take it home. What does it remind you of? What is it designed to do? Think of alternative associations—and perhaps a new invention.

ONE PRODUCT + ANOTHER PRODUCT = ONE NEW INVENTION

It has been said that there is nothing new under the sun. Inventors believe this as much as anyone. Often a "new" invention is simply two existing products or things combined in a new and startling way.

An answering machine, for example, is a combination of a tape recorder and a telephone.

For practice, let's invent something by combining two inventions that already exist—a broom and a radio.

We will start working on our invention by listing ways the broom and the radio are different.

BROOM	RADIO
Differences	
1. It helps you do a job.	1. It entertains you.
2. It can be boring to use.	2. It is fun to use.
3. It operates manually.	3. It needs batteries or electricity to operate.

Now look at the first two items on the list. Can they be combined in some way to create something new and useful? How about a musical broom! You can imagine the ads now for this invention:

BORED WITH YOUR SWEEPING CHORES?

Dance around the room with your broom to the latest top 20 hits and make a "clean sweep." Buy a new musical broom and make sweeping a breeze!

But wait a minute! There's one problem. The third item points out that a broom needs no power source other than two hands, but a radio does. We don't want a long electric cord dragging behind the musical broom, so let's make the radio battery-operated. Both batteries and radio can easily be built into the handle of the broom. Now we're in business!

INSTANT EXERCISE

Select two items from the list below. Write down their differences and find a way to combine the items into an invention that is uniquely useful.

briefcase	watch	dictionary	comb
skates	telephone	fishing pole	car
robot	toothbrush	sweater	radio

CHAPTER 7
What's a Patent?

You've read the word *patent* several times in this book. Just what is a patent and why is it so important for an inventor to have one?

A patent is more than a sheet of paper with a gold seal and a red ribbon. It is a contract between you and the United States government in which you agree to make public all the details of your invention. In exchange, the government agrees to protect your rights as the inventor. The patent gives you—and only you—control of your invention for a certain number of years. It allows you to decide who can use your invention, who can manufacture it, and who can sell it. Without a patent, you could not prevent people from copying your invention and making money from it.

To qualify for a patent, an invention must be workable, new, and useful. It also must not be obvious to anyone skilled in the field of the invention. For example an inventor probably could not patent a small lawn mower. Anyone in the business of lawn care would be able to imagine or "invent" a smaller mower.

French sculptor Frédéric Bartholdi submitted this drawing with his application for a design patent for the Statue of Liberty.

A door reflects part of the office complex at the Patent and Trademark Office.

Most patents fall into three categories: *utility patents, design patents,* and *plant patents.* Most inventions are given a patent in the utility category. This category covers everything mechanical and electrical, from a pencil sharpener to a laser writer.

A design patent is given for a design, or for styling. In 1879, Frédéric-Auguste Bartholdi of Paris, France, received a design patent on a work he had created for the United States. It was none other than our Statue of Liberty.

A plant patent is given for any new variety of flower, vegetable, or tree. People who crossbreed plants—combine one plant with another to get a new plant—are inventors, too.

Imagine now that you have invented a computerized machine. Your machine comes with a tape on which a pet owner can record sounds that are familiar and comforting to his or her pet. You call your invention the Pet Home Companion. Its purpose is to keep pets from being lonesome while their owners are away. There are millions of pet owners in the United States and you feel your invention could be useful to many people. But before you apply for a patent, you want to make sure no one else has already patented your idea.

So you pay a visit to one of the 62 patent libraries in the United States. These libraries keep files of U.S. patents. In the library you look for patented inventions that are similar to the Pet Home Companion and find none. Convinced that you have a patentable invention that is not already on the market, you think you should apply for a patent.

Not every inventor does this. Some inventors choose to put off getting a patent until they have a buyer for their invention. The buyer can often help pay the expenses of applying for and getting a patent. And some inventors simply don't bother with a patent at all. But by making an invention public for over a year without getting a patent, an inventor leaves his work unprotected.

You decide to make your application. Patents involve complex legal procedures, so you hire a patent lawyer to help you. Together, you and your lawyer prepare a patent application.

The Public Search Room of the Patent and Trademark Office contains 27 million patent references listed by subject matter.

You describe your invention in writing and draw an illustration of it. You tell how you think people will benefit from this invention. You include all the dated and witnessed records you kept while you were inventing. If someone comes along and claims to have invented the same thing, your records will show exactly when you got your idea for the Pet Home Companion and when and how you worked on it.

When your patent application is complete, you mail it to the Patent and Trademark Office (PTO) in Washington, D.C. Your application is one of thousands delivered each week to the PTO. It ends up on the desk of one of PTO's 1,400 patent examiners, who specializes in computer-controlled inventions such as yours.

The examiner reads your application thoroughly and then goes to the Search Room, where nearly every U.S. patent ever granted is on file.

Everyone at the PTO calls the Search Room files "shoes." The term goes back to the days of Thomas Jefferson. Jefferson, who was an enthusiastic inventor as well as our third president, kept his ideas for inventions in shoe boxes.

The examiner goes directly to the shoes that hold patents for recording machines like yours. It takes an expert to know where to find them, because there are 314,000 shoes stacked in 400 cases holding more than 12 million documents!

The examiner selects the documents about inventions similar to yours and studies them carefully. If there is another patented invention just like yours, you will not be granted a patent.

After weeks of work and research, the examiner decides that the Pet Home Companion is original and useful. However, he rejects your application for a patent on the grounds that your invention does not work.

You get the bad news. But you insist your invention *does* work because you used it on a recent weekend when you left your cat home alone.

The stack area of the Search Room.

The Official Gazette of the United States Patent and Trademark Office *is published once a week.*

The examiner asks you to come into his office with your machine. He switches on the Pet Home Companion and listens intently to the recorded sounds making comforting noises for your cat.

With a puzzled expression, the examiner takes apart your machine to find out how it works. Inside he discovers a small part that you had left out of the drawing on your patent application. It's back to the drawing board for you!

About a year after you file your corrected application, you receive the news that's music to every inventor's ears: "Your invention has been granted a patent."

As are all newly patented inventions, the Pet Home Companion is described in the *Official Gazette of the United States Patent and Trademark Office,* a publication that the PTO puts out every Tuesday at noon. Your invention is included along with approximately 1,500 new inventions that were issued patents the previous week.

Businessmen and manufacturers looking for new inventions might see your Pet Home Companion in the *Gazette* and decide it is just the kind of product they would like to make and sell. But don't count on that happening. You will probably have to go out and be your own salesperson.

Your patent means your invention is yours to own and you can take a bow as a serious inventor. But it alone will not bring you fame and fortune. Those rewards can come only after you've found a buyer for your invention.

The United States of America

The Commissioner of Patents and Trademarks

Has received an application for a patent for a new and useful invention. The title and description of the invention are enclosed. The requirements of law have been complied with, and it has been determined that a patent on the invention shall be granted under the law.

Therefore, this

United States Patent

Grants to the person or persons having title to this patent the right to exclude others from making, using or selling the invention throughout the United States of America for the term of seventeen years from the date of this patent, subject to the payment of maintenance fees as provided by law.

Commissioner of Patents and Trademarks—Designate

Attest

An official patent grant is awarded to those inventors whose applications have been approved. Affixed with a handsome gold seal and red ribbon, the document grants protection to the patent owner.

CHAPTER 8
Selling Your Invention

A writer once pointed out that the two most important words in an inventor's vocabulary are both Greek—*Eureka!* ("I found it!") and *Epolisa!* ("I sold it!")

Inventing something can be fun, but it's also satisfying to find someone who will pay you for all your time and effort.

How do you go about selling your invention? Well, let's start again with another imaginary invention—a pocket-sized computer and printer for people too lazy to write their own postcards while on vacation. We'll call it Comp-A-Card.

Here's how it works. A person types the names and addresses of friends on the computer, and the machine prints them on individual postcards. Vacationers then type a personal message: *Having a wonderful time. Too bad you're not here.* Each new message is added to the computer's memory bank and can be drawn on again in the future.

You are convinced that Comp-A-Card would sell well at resorts throughout the country. But first you have to find a way to get your invention mass-produced. You have two options. You could start your own business to make and sell Comp-A-Card. Or you could find a company that would buy your invention, make and sell the product, and handle all the business details.

It doesn't take you long to decide which option to take. You're an inventor, not a businessperson. So you set out to find a company that will make and market your invention for you.

Where do you start your search? Well, the Yellow Pages in your phone book are handy. They list companies by category. Match up your invention with companies that might be able to sell your product. Another helpful volume is the *Thomas Register,* which lists American companies by the products they make and sell. Any public library should have a copy of this important book.

You make a list of the companies that might be interested in buying Comp-A-Card. You write a letter to the director of new products at each company and include a description of your invention. If you already have a patent, you send along a copy of the page from the *Official Gazette* where Comp-A-Card is described. You might even include a postcard printed by your computer.

A week later, one of the companies you contacted writes back to express interest in your invention! A meeting is set up. You hire a lawyer to help you work out a legal agreement with the company.

Inventors Beware!

There are people who might want to take advantage of your invention. Get legal advice before you talk to anyone about selling your invention or before signing a contract.

The company wants to buy your invention and it gives you a choice of sales agreements: You can sell your idea for a flat fee or for a royalty.

Now here comes a tough decision. If you choose the flat fee, the company will pay you one lump sum for the right to make and sell your invention. If you choose the royalty, the company will give you a part, or percentage, of the purchase price of each Comp-A-Card it sells.

Either way you decide, some risk is involved. If Comp-A-Card is a winner, you could make a bundle with a royalty agreement. But if your invention fizzles in the marketplace, your royalty won't amount to much and you'd have been better off taking a flat fee.

As the inventor of Comp-A-Card, you may not become the world's youngest millionaire. But keep trying. You've read about young inventors of the past and the present in this book. You have curiosity, imagination, confidence, and the willingness to work at solving problems. And now you know how inventors think, where they get their ideas, and how they turn their ideas into reality. You're ready to—be an inventor!

What will you think of next?

CHAPTER 9
More Help With Inventions

INVENTORS' GROUPS

There are inventors' groups throughout the country that offer seminars, newsletters, and other services to inventors. Here is a sampling:

- American Society of Inventors, 23 Palisades Avenue, Absecon, NJ 08207
- Appalachian Inventors Group, P.O. Box 388, Oak Ridge, TN 37830 (holds an annual inventors' show)
- California Inventors Council, P.O. Box 2096, Sunnyvale, CA 94087
- Inventors' Association of New England, P.O. Box 3110, Cambridge, MA 02139
- Inventors Workshop International, 121 North Fir Street, Ventura, CA 91003 (holds an annual inventors' show)
- Midwestern Inventors Society, P.O. Box 335, St. Cloud, MN 56301
- National Congress of Inventor Organizations, P.O. Box 158, Rheem Valley, CA 94570
- Northwest Inventors Association, 723 East Highland Drive, Arlington, WA 98223
- Society of American Inventors, P.O. Box 7284, Charlotte, NC 28217

INVENTORS SHOWS

These are good places to meet inventors, attend conferences, and see new inventions on display. Some of the larger shows are:

- Cleveland Engineering Society, 3100 Chester Street, Cleveland, OH 44114
- Mid-American New Ideas Fair, P.O. Box 100, Hills City, KS 67642
- Minnesota Inventors Congress, P.O. Box 71, Redwood Falls, MN 56283
- National Inventors Show, New York Hilton Hotel, Avenue of the Americas at 53d Street, New York, NY 10019

ASSOCIATIONS

For legal help with an invention, write to:

- American Patent Law Association, 2001 Jefferson Davis Highway, Arlington, VA 22202
- Patent Office Society, Box 2089, Arlington, VA 22202

For information on patents, Depository Libraries, people who prepare patent applications, and National Inventors' Week, held every February, as well as information on protecting your idea by using the Document Disclosure Program, write to:

- Patent and Trademark Office, Washington, DC 20231

Suggested Reading

Abernathy, David and Wayne Knipe. *Ideas, Inventions and Patents.* Pioneer Press, P.O. Box 76025, Atlanta, Georgia 30328.

Adams, James L. *Conceptual Blockbusting—A Guide to Better Ideas.* W. H. Freeman and Company, San Francisco, California, 1974.

American Bar Association. *What is a Patent?* Circulation Department, 1155 East 60th Street, Chicago, Illinois, 1982.

American Heritage (eds.). *Men of Science and Invention.* American Heritage Publishing, New York, 1960.

American Patent Law Association. *How to Protect and Benefit From Your Ideas.* 2001 Jefferson Davis Highway, Arlington, Virginia 22202, 1981.

Burke, James. *Connections.* Little, Brown & Co., Boston, 1978.

Giscard d'Estaing, Valerie-Anne. *The World Almanac Book of Inventions.* Ballantine Books/Random House, New York, 1985.

Green, Orville N. and Frank L. Durr, with John Berseth. *Practical Inventors Handbook.* McGraw-Hill, New York, 1979.

Heyn, Ernest V. *Fire of Genius.* Anchor Press/Doubleday, Garden City, 1976.

International Entrepreneurs' Association. *How to Test Market Your Ideas and Products.* 631 Wilshire Boulevard, Santa Monica, California 90401.

Kivenson, Gilbert. *The Art and Science of Inventing.* Van Nostrand & Reinhold, New York, 1977.

Mueller, Robert E. *Inventivity: How Man Creates in Art and Science.* John Day Company, New York, 1963.

Robertson, Patrick. *The Book of Firsts.* Clarkson N. Potter, Inc., New York, 1974.

Small Business Administration. *Small Business Bibliographies.* P.O. Box 15434, Fort Worth, Texas 76119.

Smithsonian Exposition Books. *The Smithsonian Book of Invention.* W. W. Norton & Co., New York, 1978.

White, Richard M., Jr. *The Entrepreneur's Manual.* Chilton Book Company, Radnor, Pennsylvania, 1977.

The books on the previous page are only a partial listing of titles that will give you background on inventors and inventions. Check the card catalog of your library for other suggestions. But reading only books will not keep you abreast of the newest and latest developments in the world of inventions. To stay up-to-date on inventions, you should read articles in current magazines, journals, and other periodicals. *The Readers' Guide to Periodical Literature* is a valuable reference work that lists articles alphabetically by subject areas and the periodicals in which they appear. The *Guide* also tells you the author of each article, which issue it appears in, and page numbers. Look for this helpful book in the reference section of your school or local library. Once you have written down the articles you would like to read, the librarian can help you locate the particular issues in which the articles appear.

ACKNOWLEDGMENTS

Thanks are due to the many people whose contributions helped make this book possible. Special recognition should go to the U.S. Patent and Trademark Office, and particularly Oscar Mastin for technical advice and assistance; Charles F. Schroeder, patent attorney, for advice and encouragement; Diane D'Andrade and Elizabeth Zuraw, editors, respectively, at Harcourt Brace Jovanovich and Weekly Reader Books, for shepherding the book through to publication; Nancy Norton, Senior Designer, Weekly Reader Books, for coordinating all art and design; Steven Otfinoski, for rewrite of the final version of the manuscript; Louise Augeri and Mary Ellen Renn, for photo research; Barbara Jean Dooley and Noël Higgins, for copyreading; Marian Canedo of the Buffalo Invention Program, for stimulating the interest of *Weekly Reader* in an invention program; Stuart Krichevsky of Sterling Lord-Literistic, Inc., for recognizing the potential for a book on the subject; and the more than 300,000 children whose participation in the invention contests have provided continuous inspiration to everyone working on the book.

ANSWERS

Pages **19–21**

A. HUNTING DECOY
Designed to help hunters outsmart ducks and other flying game, this grazing cow is actually camouflage for two hunters. When the hunters are ready to fire, they lower the neck of the decoy or open a panel on its side.

B. FOOTWEAR WITH HEEL AND TOE POSITIONS REVERSED
The toes of these soldier's boots point in the opposite direction from that in which they're actually moving. Because the boots point backward when the soldier walks forward, they give the enemy the impression that its foe is headed another way.

C. AMBULATORY SLEEPING BAG
This unique sleeping bag is called ambulatory because it lets a camper move about. It has openings for arms and legs, allowing a camper, while snug inside the bag, to scratch an itchy nose or to take off in a hurry from a wandering bear.

D. IMPROVEMENT IN FIRE ESCAPES
This invention helps people save themselves from burning buildings. A person attaches the five-foot-wide parachute to his or her head, neck, or arms before leaping from the burning building. With the parachute, the person can land safely, while pads on the soles of the shoes cushion the shock.

E. SPAGHETTI FORK
This spinning fork is intended to make a favorite food easier to eat. The diner turns on the switch and a motor spins the tines, wrapping strands of spaghetti neatly around the fork.

Page **57**